Understanding BPD: A Resource Guide for Families and Friends

Mila Georgiev

Chapter 1

Understanding Borderline Personality Disorder

Definition and Overview

Borderline Personality Disorder (BPD) is a complex mental health condition characterized by pervasive patterns of instability in interpersonal relationships, self-image, and emotions. Individuals with BPD often experience intense emotional responses, leading to difficulties in managing feelings such as anger, sadness, and anxiety. This emotional volatility can result in impulsive behaviors, relationship conflicts, and challenges in maintaining a stable sense of self. Understanding BPD is crucial for those affected by it, as well as for their families, friends, and mental health professionals who seek to provide support and guidance.

Understanding BPD: A Resource Guide for Families and Friends

The symptoms of BPD frequently manifest in several key areas. Affected individuals may struggle with intense fear of abandonment, leading to frantic efforts to avoid real or imagined separation. This fear can drive impulsive actions, such as sudden changes in relationships or self-destructive behaviors. Additionally, individuals with BPD often exhibit difficulties in regulating their emotions, which can result in rapid mood swings and feelings of emptiness. These symptoms contribute to a cycle of instability that can affect personal and professional relationships, making it essential to address not only the disorder itself but also the coping strategies that can aid in emotional regulation.

Coping strategies play a vital role in managing BPD and improving quality of life. Techniques such as mindfulness and meditation can help individuals focus on the present moment, reducing anxiety and emotional turmoil. Nutrition and meal planning also emerge as significant factors, as a balanced diet can positively influence mood and overall well-being. Moreover, engaging in creative therapies allows for self-expression and healing, providing alternative avenues for individuals to process their emotions constructively. These strategies can empower those with BPD to navigate their daily challenges more effectively.

Understanding BPD: A Resource Guide for Families and Friends

Building healthy relationships is another critical aspect of managing BPD. Individuals with this disorder often grapple with trust and attachment issues, which can hinder their ability to form stable connections. Learning communication skills and establishing boundaries are essential steps for creating and maintaining healthy interactions. Support systems, including family, friends, and community resources, play a crucial role in providing the necessary encouragement and understanding. Mental health professionals can facilitate this process, guiding individuals toward healthier relational dynamics.

Finally, navigating therapy options is fundamental for individuals with BPD, as tailored therapeutic approaches can significantly enhance recovery. Various modalities, such as Dialectical Behavior Therapy (DBT), focus on teaching emotional regulation skills and interpersonal effectiveness. Additionally, addressing co-occurring disorders, such as depression or anxiety, is essential for comprehensive treatment. Educational resources for families and friends can further bridge the gap between understanding BPD and providing meaningful support. By fostering a supportive environment, individuals with BPD can embark on a path toward healing and stability.

Symptoms and Diagnosis

Borderline Personality Disorder (BPD) is characterized by a range of emotional, behavioral, and relational symptoms that can significantly affect an individual's daily life. Common symptoms include intense emotional instability, impulsive behavior, a distorted self-image, and difficulties in maintaining stable relationships. Individuals with BPD often experience rapid mood swings that can last from a few hours to a few days. These emotional fluctuations can be triggered by external events or internal thoughts, leading to feelings of emptiness and difficulty in regulating emotions. Recognizing these symptoms is crucial for individuals and their loved ones to navigate the complexities of BPD effectively.

Diagnosis of BPD typically involves a comprehensive evaluation by a mental health professional, which may include clinical interviews, self-report questionnaires, and discussions of personal and family medical histories. The Diagnostic and Statistical Manual of Mental Disorders (DSM-5) outlines specific criteria for diagnosing BPD, including patterns of unstable relationships, fear of abandonment, and self-destructive behaviors. Mental health professionals look for these patterns to differentiate BPD from other mental health disorders that may present similar symptoms, ensuring an accurate diagnosis. Early diagnosis can lead to more effective treatment strategies and coping mechanisms.

Understanding BPD: A Resource Guide for Families and Friends

Understanding the nuances of BPD symptoms is essential for families and friends who may witness the challenges faced by their loved ones. They may notice behaviors such as self-harm, substance abuse, or risky activities, which can be alarming and confusing. Open communication and education about BPD can foster a supportive environment where individuals feel understood rather than judged. It is important for family members to recognize that these behaviors are often manifestations of deeper emotional pain rather than deliberate attempts to cause harm. This understanding can help them respond with empathy and patience, ultimately facilitating healthier interactions.

Coping strategies play a vital role in managing the symptoms of BPD. Individuals can benefit from learning emotional regulation techniques, such as mindfulness and meditation, which can help them become more aware of their feelings and triggers. Establishing a routine that includes balanced nutrition and meal planning can also contribute to better emotional stability. Furthermore, creative therapies, like art or music therapy, can provide an outlet for self-expression, allowing individuals to process their emotions in a constructive way. These strategies not only enhance personal well-being but also promote healthier relationships with those around them.

Understanding BPD: A Resource Guide for Families and Friends

For individuals with BPD and their support systems, accessing community resources and support networks is crucial. Therapies tailored specifically for BPD, such as Dialectical Behavior Therapy (DBT), can provide structured approaches to managing symptoms effectively. Joining support groups can also offer invaluable connections, allowing individuals to share their experiences and coping mechanisms. Educational resources for families and friends are essential for fostering understanding and advocacy, ensuring they are equipped to support their loved ones. By building a solid foundation of knowledge and support, individuals with BPD can navigate their challenges while fostering healthier relationships and a more stable emotional landscape.

Myths and Misconceptions

Myths and misconceptions surrounding borderline personality disorder (BPD) can create significant barriers for individuals living with the condition, as well as for their families and support systems. One common myth is that people with BPD are manipulative or attention-seeking. This misconception often stems from misunderstandings around the intense emotions and behaviors characteristic of BPD. In reality, individuals with BPD often struggle with profound feelings of abandonment and emotional instability, which can lead to behaviors that appear manipulative but are actually expressions of distress. Recognizing this can foster empathy and understanding rather than judgment.

Understanding BPD: A Resource Guide for Families and Friends

Another prevalent myth is that BPD is untreatable. While BPD has historically been viewed as a challenging disorder to manage, research has shown that effective treatments are available. Dialectical behavior therapy (DBT), cognitive-behavioral therapy (CBT), and mindfulness techniques have proven beneficial for many individuals with BPD. These therapies focus on emotional regulation, interpersonal effectiveness, and distress tolerance skills, enabling individuals to lead fulfilling lives. By debunking the notion that recovery is impossible, we can encourage those with BPD to seek help and support.

Some people believe that BPD only affects women, but this is another misconception that overlooks the experiences of men and non-binary individuals. Though BPD is diagnosed more frequently in women, it is important to understand that men can also experience the disorder. The symptoms may manifest differently, and societal norms about masculinity can lead to underdiagnosis or misdiagnosis in men. Broadening the understanding of BPD to include all genders can help ensure that everyone receives appropriate care and support.

Understanding BPD: A Resource Guide for Families and Friends

The idea that individuals with BPD are inherently dangerous or violent is another harmful myth. While emotional dysregulation can lead to impulsive actions, it does not equate to violent behavior. Most individuals with BPD are not a threat to others; rather, they often struggle with their own emotional turmoil and may even have a heightened sensitivity to the emotions of those around them. Education on this topic can help dispel fear and promote a more compassionate view of individuals living with BPD, fostering healthier relationships.

Lastly, some believe that family and friends of individuals with BPD should simply "toughen up" or learn to ignore the behaviors associated with the disorder. This misconception can lead to isolation and guilt among loved ones, who often feel overwhelmed and unsure of how to support their family member. It is crucial for families and friends to understand that they are not alone and that support systems exist to help them navigate the complexities of BPD. Resources, such as educational materials and community support groups, can provide valuable insights and coping strategies, ultimately leading to healthier relationships and improved emotional well-being for everyone involved.

Understanding BPD: A Resource Guide for Families and Friends

Understanding BPD: A Resource Guide for Families and Friends

Chapter 2

Coping Strategies for Emotional Regulation

Identifying Triggers

Identifying triggers is a crucial step in understanding and managing borderline personality disorder (BPD). Triggers are specific situations, events, or stimuli that provoke strong emotional responses, often leading to distressing symptoms such as anger, anxiety, or sadness. Recognizing these triggers enables individuals with BPD, as well as their families and friends, to create effective coping strategies, thereby facilitating emotional regulation. By keeping a detailed journal of emotions and experiences, individuals can begin to identify patterns related to their triggers, which may include interpersonal conflicts, feelings of abandonment, or situations that amplify fear or inadequacy.

Understanding BPD: A Resource Guide for Families and Friends

Common triggers for individuals with BPD can stem from various sources, including personal relationships, environmental factors, and internal thoughts. For instance, conflict with loved ones may evoke feelings of abandonment or fear of loss, while certain social situations may heighten feelings of inadequacy or rejection. Internal triggers may manifest as negative self-talk or memories of past traumas. It's important for both individuals with BPD and their support systems to recognize that triggers can vary widely from person to person and may change over time. Understanding this variability allows for more tailored approaches to coping and emotional regulation.

Mindfulness and meditation techniques can be particularly effective in helping individuals identify their triggers. Through practices such as mindful breathing and body scans, individuals can cultivate greater awareness of their thoughts and feelings as they arise. This heightened awareness can provide valuable insights into potential triggers, enabling proactive responses rather than reactive ones. Additionally, engaging in creative therapies, such as art or music therapy, can offer alternative avenues for self-expression, making it easier to explore and articulate feelings associated with specific triggers.

Understanding BPD: A Resource Guide for Families and Friends

Building a supportive environment is also essential for identifying triggers. Family and friends play a pivotal role in this process by fostering open communication and creating a safe space for discussions about emotions and experiences. Supportive relationships can encourage individuals with BPD to share their triggers without fear of judgment, leading to a better understanding of these emotional responses. Furthermore, involving mental health professionals in this journey can provide additional tools and strategies for both individuals and their support systems, enhancing their ability to navigate triggers effectively.

Lastly, education about BPD and its associated triggers is vital for families, friends, and mental health professionals. By equipping themselves with knowledge about the disorder, they can better understand the complexities of emotional regulation and the role triggers play in the lives of individuals with BPD. This understanding can lead to more compassionate interactions and the development of effective coping strategies tailored to each unique situation. Recognizing and identifying triggers is not merely about managing symptoms; it is about fostering healthier relationships and promoting a greater sense of stability in the lives of those affected by BPD.

Practical Techniques for Emotional Stability

Practical techniques for emotional stability are essential for individuals with borderline personality disorder (BPD) and their support systems. Emotional instability is a hallmark of BPD, often leading to intense feelings that can be overwhelming and difficult to manage. Developing effective coping strategies can help individuals regulate their emotions and reduce the frequency and intensity of emotional crises. Techniques such as grounding exercises, cognitive restructuring, and developing a personalized coping toolkit can empower individuals to gain control over their emotional responses and create a sense of stability in their daily lives.

Nutrition plays a crucial role in emotional well-being, and meal planning can significantly impact mood and emotional regulation. A balanced diet that includes essential nutrients can support brain health and overall emotional stability. Individuals with BPD may benefit from working with a nutritionist to create a meal plan that emphasizes whole foods, omega-3 fatty acids, and a regular eating schedule. Additionally, staying hydrated and reducing caffeine and sugar intake can help mitigate mood swings. By prioritizing nutrition, individuals can foster a stronger connection between their physical health and emotional stability.

Understanding BPD: A Resource Guide for Families and Friends

Mindfulness and meditation techniques are particularly effective for those with BPD, as they promote self-awareness and emotional regulation. Mindfulness practices encourage individuals to stay present, observe their thoughts and feelings without judgment, and create a space between stimuli and reactions. Techniques such as guided meditation, deep breathing exercises, and body scans can help individuals cultivate a sense of calm and centeredness. Regular practice can enhance emotional resilience and provide individuals with tools to navigate the emotional turbulence characteristic of BPD.

Building healthy relationships is another critical aspect of achieving emotional stability. Effective communication skills, such as active listening and expressing needs assertively, can foster more supportive interactions. Setting healthy boundaries is equally important, as it ensures that individuals maintain their sense of self while engaging with others. Support groups and therapy can provide a safe environment for practicing these skills, helping individuals to develop connections that nurture rather than deplete their emotional resources. Healthy relationships are foundational for emotional stability and can serve as a buffer against the challenges of living with BPD.

Creative therapies offer an innovative approach to self-expression and healing for individuals with BPD. Engaging in art, music, or writing can provide a constructive outlet for emotions that may be difficult to verbalize. These activities can facilitate emotional release and insight, helping individuals process their feelings in a non-threatening manner. Additionally, creative therapies can enhance self-esteem and promote a sense of accomplishment, both of which are vital for emotional stability. Exploring various creative avenues can encourage individuals to discover new aspects of themselves, ultimately contributing to healthier emotional regulation and a more fulfilling life.

Long-term Strategies for Regulation

Long-term strategies for regulation in individuals with borderline personality disorder (BPD) focus on cultivating sustainable practices that promote emotional stability and resilience over time. Understanding the nature of BPD and its impact on emotional regulation is crucial for both individuals with the disorder and their support systems. By implementing long-term strategies, individuals can better manage their emotional responses, leading to healthier relationships and improved overall well-being.

Understanding BPD: A Resource Guide for Families and Friends

One effective long-term strategy is the integration of mindfulness and meditation techniques into daily routines. Mindfulness practices help individuals become more aware of their thoughts and feelings without judgment, enabling them to observe emotional fluctuations and respond more thoughtfully. Simple exercises, such as deep breathing or guided meditations, can be incorporated into everyday life, providing a foundation for emotional regulation. As individuals build their mindfulness skills, they often find it easier to navigate overwhelming emotions, reducing the likelihood of impulsive reactions.

Nutrition and meal planning also play a significant role in emotional regulation. A well-balanced diet can positively affect mood and energy levels, contributing to overall mental health. Individuals with BPD may benefit from working with a nutritionist to develop a meal plan that includes a variety of nutrients, such as omega-3 fatty acids, which are known to support brain health. Establishing regular meal times and incorporating healthy snacks can help stabilize blood sugar levels, further aiding emotional regulation. By prioritizing nutrition, individuals can create a supportive environment for managing their emotions.

Understanding BPD: A Resource Guide for Families and Friends

Building healthy relationships is another vital strategy for long-term regulation. Individuals with BPD often experience intense emotions that can strain relationships. Developing communication skills, such as active listening and expressing needs clearly, can foster understanding and support among family and friends. Support systems, including therapy groups or community resources, can also provide safe spaces for individuals to share experiences and learn from others facing similar challenges. By nurturing these connections, individuals can cultivate a sense of belonging and reduce feelings of isolation.

Lastly, engaging in creative therapies offers a unique avenue for self-expression and healing. Art, music, and writing can serve as powerful tools for individuals with BPD to process emotions and experiences. Creative outlets not only provide a distraction during difficult times but also facilitate a deeper understanding of one's feelings. By incorporating creative therapies into their lives, individuals can enhance their emotional regulation skills and build a more positive self-image. These long-term strategies, when combined, create a comprehensive approach to managing BPD, leading to improved emotional health and stronger interpersonal relationships.

Understanding BPD: A Resource Guide for Families and Friends

Understanding BPD: A Resource Guide for Families and Friends

Chapter 3

Nutrition and Meal Planning

Importance of Nutrition in Mental Health

Nutrition plays a crucial role in mental health, particularly for individuals with borderline personality disorder (BPD). A balanced diet can significantly influence mood regulation, cognitive function, and overall emotional stability. For those with BPD, where emotional dysregulation is a core symptom, understanding how nutrients affect the brain can empower individuals and their loved ones to make informed choices about food. Nutritional deficiencies can exacerbate mental health issues, making it essential to prioritize a well-rounded diet that supports brain health.

Understanding BPD: A Resource Guide for Families and Friends

Essential fatty acids, such as omega-3s found in fish, flaxseed, and walnuts, have been shown to improve mood and reduce symptoms of anxiety and depression. These nutrients contribute to the structure and function of brain cells, enhancing communication between them. For individuals with BPD, incorporating omega-3-rich foods can provide a natural approach to managing emotional instability. Additionally, the consumption of whole grains, lean proteins, and a variety of fruits and vegetables can help stabilize blood sugar levels, which plays a critical role in maintaining mood and energy throughout the day.

Moreover, certain vitamins and minerals are vital for optimal brain function. For instance, B vitamins, particularly B6, B12, and folate, are essential for neurotransmitter production, which directly affects mood regulation. A deficiency in these vitamins may lead to increased irritability and depressive symptoms. Therefore, individuals with BPD and their support systems should consider focusing on nutrient-dense foods that provide these essential vitamins, such as leafy greens, legumes, eggs, and fortified cereals. Meal planning that includes these foods can be a proactive strategy for emotional well-being.

Understanding BPD: A Resource Guide for Families and Friends

Mindfulness and meditation practices can be enriched by the incorporation of nutrition. The act of preparing and consuming meals can serve as a mindful practice, allowing individuals to focus on the present moment and engage fully with their food. This connection between nutrition and mindfulness can foster a greater awareness of how different foods impact mood and emotional states. Encouraging individuals with BPD to explore this relationship may enhance their coping strategies and contribute to improved emotional regulation.

Building a supportive community around healthy eating can also be beneficial. Family members and friends can play an active role by participating in meal planning and preparation, creating an environment that values nutrition as a component of mental health. Sharing recipes, cooking together, and discussing the benefits of various foods can strengthen relationships and promote a collective commitment to wellness. As individuals with BPD navigate their challenges, having a solid support system that emphasizes the importance of nutrition can be a valuable resource in their journey towards emotional stability and healing.

Meal Planning Basics

Meal planning is an essential practice for individuals with borderline personality disorder (BPD) as it can significantly aid in emotional regulation and overall well-being. Establishing a structured meal plan helps create a sense of stability and predictability, which can be particularly beneficial for those who often experience emotional dysregulation. By planning meals in advance, individuals can make healthier food choices and avoid impulsive eating behaviors that may stem from emotional distress. This proactive approach allows for better management of both physical and mental health, providing a solid foundation for coping strategies.

When developing a meal plan, it is important to consider nutritional balance. A well-rounded diet should include a variety of food groups: fruits, vegetables, whole grains, lean proteins, and healthy fats. Each of these components plays a crucial role in maintaining energy levels and supporting brain health. For example, omega-3 fatty acids found in fish and flaxseeds are linked to improved mood regulation. Incorporating these nutrient-rich foods can help mitigate some of the emotional symptoms associated with BPD, making it easier to navigate daily challenges.

Mindfulness can be a powerful tool in the meal planning process. Taking the time to engage in mindful eating practices allows individuals to develop a deeper awareness of their body's hunger cues and emotional triggers. This can involve savoring each bite, paying attention to the flavors and textures of food, and recognizing feelings of fullness. By integrating mindfulness into meal planning and eating, individuals with BPD can cultivate a more positive relationship with food, reducing the likelihood of using eating as a coping mechanism during times of emotional turmoil.

In addition to personal benefits, meal planning can also foster healthier relationships with family and friends. When individuals with BPD involve their loved ones in the meal planning process, it can create opportunities for connection and communication. Preparing meals together can serve as a bonding experience, providing a platform for discussing feelings and struggles in a supportive environment. Furthermore, sharing meals that have been thoughtfully prepared can help reinforce a sense of community and belonging, both of which are vital for emotional well-being.

Finally, utilizing community resources can enhance the meal planning experience. Many organizations offer nutrition workshops, cooking classes, and support groups tailored to those with BPD or mental health concerns. These resources can provide valuable information on meal planning while fostering connections with others who share similar experiences. By seeking out these opportunities, individuals can build a supportive network that not only aids in meal planning but also contributes to their overall journey of healing and self-discovery.

Foods to Incorporate and Avoid

Foods play a crucial role in emotional regulation, particularly for individuals with borderline personality disorder (BPD). Incorporating nutrient-dense foods into the diet can help stabilize mood and improve overall mental health. Foods rich in omega-3 fatty acids, such as salmon, walnuts, and flaxseeds, have been shown to reduce symptoms of depression and anxiety. These healthy fats support brain function and can enhance emotional regulation. Additionally, complex carbohydrates found in whole grains, legumes, and vegetables can help increase serotonin levels in the brain, contributing to a more positive mood.

Understanding BPD: A Resource Guide for Families and Friends

In contrast, certain foods and substances may exacerbate symptoms associated with BPD. Highly processed foods, which are often high in sugars and unhealthy fats, can lead to mood swings and irritability. Caffeine and alcohol can also have detrimental effects, as they may increase anxiety and disrupt sleep patterns. For individuals with BPD, it is advisable to limit or avoid these substances to promote emotional stability. Instead, focusing on whole, unprocessed foods can create a more balanced diet that supports mental health.

Mindfulness and meditation techniques can be enhanced by dietary choices. Engaging in mindful eating practices can help individuals with BPD develop a healthier relationship with food. Taking the time to savor each bite, recognizing hunger cues, and appreciating the flavors can foster a sense of control and presence. This practice not only promotes better digestion but also encourages emotional awareness, which is essential for managing BPD symptoms. Incorporating mindfulness into meal planning can also lead to healthier choices and reduce impulsive eating behaviors.

Understanding BPD: A Resource Guide for Families and Friends

Building healthy relationships while managing BPD can be supported by nutritional choices. Sharing meals with family and friends can create bonding experiences and foster open communication. Cooking together can also serve as a therapeutic activity, allowing individuals to express themselves creatively while reinforcing social connections. Encouraging loved ones to participate in healthy meal planning can help create a supportive environment that prioritizes emotional well-being. This collaborative approach can strengthen relationships and provide a crucial support system for individuals navigating the challenges of BPD.

Education about nutrition and its impact on mental health is essential for families and friends of those with BPD. Understanding the connection between diet and emotional regulation can empower loved ones to support healthy habits. Providing resources on meal planning, cooking classes, or nutrition workshops can enhance the overall well-being of those affected by BPD. By fostering an environment that encourages healthy eating and emotional support, families and friends can play an integral role in the healing journey of individuals with borderline personality disorder.

Understanding BPD: A Resource Guide for Families and Friends

Understanding BPD: A Resource Guide for Families and Friends

Chapter 4

Mindfulness and Meditation Techniques

Introduction to Mindfulness

Mindfulness is a practice that encompasses being present in the moment, acknowledging one's thoughts and feelings without judgment, and cultivating a sense of awareness towards oneself and the environment. For individuals with borderline personality disorder (BPD), incorporating mindfulness into daily life can be an effective strategy for emotional regulation, reducing impulsivity, and managing intense feelings. This practice encourages a gentle observation of one's internal experiences, allowing individuals to create distance from overwhelming emotions that often accompany BPD. By fostering mindfulness, individuals can develop a greater understanding of their emotional triggers and responses, leading to healthier coping mechanisms.

Understanding BPD: A Resource Guide for Families and Friends

The application of mindfulness techniques can significantly benefit those experiencing the tumultuous emotional landscape of BPD. Techniques such as focused breathing, body scans, and mindful observation can help ground individuals during moments of distress. These practices not only promote relaxation but also enhance self-awareness, enabling individuals to recognize when they are entering a state of emotional dysregulation. This heightened awareness is crucial, as it allows for timely interventions, whether through self-soothing techniques or reaching out for support from loved ones or professionals.

Incorporating mindfulness into nutrition and meal planning can further enhance its benefits for individuals with BPD. Mindful eating encourages individuals to savor their meals, paying attention to flavors, textures, and the body's hunger cues. This approach can foster a healthier relationship with food and body image, reducing the likelihood of impulsive eating behaviors that may stem from emotional distress. By practicing mindfulness during meals, individuals can cultivate a sense of control and awareness that translates into other areas of their lives, ultimately leading to improved emotional regulation.

Understanding BPD: A Resource Guide for Families and Friends

Building healthy relationships is another area where mindfulness can play a transformative role. Mindful communication involves active listening, empathy, and openness, which are essential components for nurturing connections with others. For family and friends of individuals with BPD, practicing mindfulness can enhance their understanding and compassion towards their loved ones' experiences. By remaining present during interactions, they can respond more thoughtfully rather than reactively, creating a supportive environment where individuals with BPD feel validated and understood. This mutual practice of mindfulness can strengthen relationships and foster a sense of community.

Creative therapies also benefit from the integration of mindfulness practices. Engaging in art, music, or movement with a mindful approach allows individuals with BPD to express their emotions in a safe and constructive manner. This form of self-expression can serve as a powerful outlet, promoting healing and reflection. By being fully present in the creative process, individuals can explore their feelings without the constraints of judgment or criticism, leading to greater emotional insight and resilience. Overall, mindfulness serves as a foundational element in navigating the complexities of BPD, offering practical tools for emotional regulation, relationship building, and personal growth.

Meditation Practices for Emotional Balance

Meditation practices can be a powerful tool for individuals seeking emotional balance, particularly for those navigating the complexities of borderline personality disorder (BPD). These practices promote mindfulness, helping individuals develop a heightened awareness of their thoughts and feelings. By incorporating meditation into daily routines, individuals with BPD can cultivate a non-judgmental attitude towards their emotions, allowing them to observe their internal experiences without becoming overwhelmed or reactive. This shift in perspective can significantly enhance emotional regulation, which is often a challenge for those with BPD.

One effective meditation technique is mindfulness meditation, which encourages individuals to focus on their breath while observing their thoughts and feelings as they arise. This practice can help in recognizing emotional triggers and patterns, fostering an understanding of how certain thoughts may lead to intense emotional reactions. By regularly engaging in mindfulness meditation, individuals can enhance their ability to remain present, reducing the likelihood of being swept away by emotional turbulence. Over time, this increased awareness can empower individuals to respond to their emotions more thoughtfully and constructively.

Understanding BPD: A Resource Guide for Families and Friends

Another useful approach is loving-kindness meditation, which emphasizes compassion towards oneself and others. This practice involves silently repeating phrases that express goodwill and kindness, both to oneself and to those around them. For individuals with BPD, who may struggle with self-criticism and feelings of unworthiness, loving-kindness meditation can serve as a gentle reminder of their inherent value. This technique not only nurtures self-acceptance but also helps in fostering healthier relationships by encouraging empathy and understanding towards others, which can be especially beneficial in managing interpersonal conflicts.

Guided imagery is another meditation practice that can be tailored to support emotional balance. This technique involves visualizing calming and peaceful scenes, which can induce a sense of tranquility and help alleviate feelings of anxiety or distress. Individuals can create personalized imagery that resonates with their experiences, allowing them to find solace in their mind's eye. By incorporating guided imagery into their routine, individuals with BPD can cultivate a safe mental space where they can retreat during times of emotional overwhelm, ultimately aiding in emotional regulation.

In conclusion, integrating meditation practices into daily life can significantly enhance emotional balance for individuals with borderline personality disorder. Whether through mindfulness meditation, loving-kindness practices, or guided imagery, these techniques provide valuable tools for fostering self-awareness, compassion, and calmness. Families, friends, and mental health professionals can support individuals in exploring these practices, encouraging consistency and patience as they work towards greater emotional stability. With commitment and practice, meditation can become a cornerstone of emotional well-being for those affected by BPD.

Incorporating Mindfulness into Daily Life

Incorporating mindfulness into daily life can significantly enhance emotional regulation for individuals with borderline personality disorder (BPD). Mindfulness is the practice of being present in the moment, which allows for greater awareness of thoughts and feelings without immediate reaction. This practice can help individuals with BPD recognize emotional triggers and develop healthier responses. Simple techniques, such as focusing on the breath or observing surroundings with intention, can create a buffer against overwhelming emotions and impulsive reactions. By integrating mindfulness into everyday routines, individuals can cultivate a sense of calm and clarity, making it easier to navigate the complexities of their emotions.

Understanding BPD: A Resource Guide for Families and Friends

One effective way to incorporate mindfulness into daily life is through structured mindfulness exercises. These can include activities such as meditation, yoga, or guided imagery. Setting aside a few minutes each day for these practices can help establish a routine that promotes self-awareness and emotional stability. For instance, a brief morning meditation can set a positive tone for the day, while an evening reflection can provide closure and insight into the day's experiences. Additionally, apps and online resources can offer guided sessions tailored to the needs of individuals with BPD, making these practices more accessible and engaging.

Mindfulness can also be woven into everyday activities, transforming routine tasks into opportunities for practice. Engaging fully in activities such as eating, walking, or even washing dishes can enhance the mindfulness experience. When eating, for example, individuals can focus on the taste, texture, and aroma of their food, which not only promotes mindful eating but also fosters a healthier relationship with food. Similarly, during a walk, paying attention to the sensations of movement and the environment can ground individuals in the present, reducing anxiety and fostering a connection to the world around them.

Understanding BPD: A Resource Guide for Families and Friends

Building a support system that encourages mindfulness can further enhance its integration into daily life. Family members and friends can play a crucial role by participating in mindfulness practices together. This shared experience not only strengthens relationships but also fosters an environment that values emotional awareness and support. Additionally, mental health professionals can incorporate mindfulness techniques into therapy sessions, providing individuals with practical tools to use outside of therapy. Encouragement and accountability from loved ones can help individuals remain committed to their mindfulness practice, reinforcing its benefits over time.

Finally, it is essential to acknowledge that mindfulness is not a one-size-fits-all solution. Individuals with BPD may need to experiment with different techniques and approaches to find what resonates best with them. Patience and self-compassion are key as individuals navigate their mindfulness journeys. By remaining open to the process and recognizing that progress may involve setbacks, individuals can cultivate resilience and a deeper understanding of themselves. Ultimately, incorporating mindfulness into daily life can lead to improved emotional regulation, enhanced relationships, and a greater sense of peace for those living with borderline personality disorder.

Understanding BPD: A Resource Guide for Families and Friends

Understanding BPD: A Resource Guide for Families and Friends

Chapter 5

Building Healthy Relationships

Understanding Relationship Dynamics

Understanding relationship dynamics is crucial for individuals with borderline personality disorder (BPD), their families, and mental health professionals. The nature of BPD often leads to intense emotional experiences, which can significantly affect interpersonal relationships. Relationships may oscillate between extremes of idealization and devaluation, creating a turbulent environment not only for the individual with BPD but also for their loved ones. Recognizing these patterns is the first step towards fostering healthier interactions and reducing relational conflict.

Emotional dysregulation is a hallmark of BPD and can complicate relationship dynamics. Individuals may struggle to manage their emotions effectively, leading to impulsive behaviors and rapid mood swings. These fluctuations can create a rollercoaster effect in relationships, where moments of closeness are often followed by feelings of abandonment or anger. Family members and friends may feel confused and helpless, unsure of how to respond to these emotional highs and lows. Understanding these triggers and responses is essential for developing empathy and patience among loved ones.

Understanding BPD: A Resource Guide for Families and Friends

Building healthy relationships while living with BPD requires effort from both the individual and their support system. Open communication plays a vital role in establishing trust and understanding. Encouraging discussions about feelings and boundaries can help clarify expectations and reduce misunderstandings. Additionally, practicing mindfulness and meditation techniques can assist individuals with BPD in regulating their emotions, allowing for more stable and constructive interactions. These practices can also help loved ones remain grounded and supportive during difficult moments.

Creative therapies can serve as an invaluable resource for self-expression and healing in the context of relationship dynamics. Engaging in art, music, or writing can provide individuals with BPD a safe outlet for their emotions, reducing the intensity of feelings that might otherwise spill over into relationships. These creative avenues not only foster self-discovery but also promote connection with others, as sharing artistic expressions can deepen bonds and enhance mutual understanding. Families and friends can participate in these activities, promoting a collaborative approach to healing.

Finally, establishing a robust support system can significantly enhance the ability to navigate relationship dynamics influenced by BPD. Community resources, support groups, and educational programs can provide both individuals with BPD and their loved ones with valuable tools and strategies for coping. These resources help all parties involved to develop better emotional regulation skills, facilitating healthier interactions. By recognizing the complexities of relationship dynamics and actively working towards improvement, individuals with BPD and their support networks can create more fulfilling, stable, and loving connections.

Communication Skills for Healthy Interactions

Effective communication skills are essential for fostering healthy interactions, particularly for individuals with borderline personality disorder (BPD) and their loved ones. Understanding how to express thoughts and feelings clearly can significantly enhance relationships and reduce misunderstandings. Active listening, a key component of effective communication, involves fully concentrating on what the other person is saying, showing empathy, and providing feedback. This practice helps validate the feelings of individuals with BPD, allowing them to feel heard and understood, which is crucial in managing emotional volatility.

Understanding BPD: A Resource Guide for Families and Friends

Nonverbal communication also plays a vital role in interactions. Body language, facial expressions, and tone of voice can convey emotions and intentions just as strongly as words. For individuals with BPD, being aware of these nonverbal cues can help in managing their responses and perceptions during conversations. Similarly, family members and friends can benefit from recognizing the nonverbal signals of their loved ones, as this awareness can lead to more compassionate and supportive interactions. By cultivating a shared understanding of nonverbal communication, relationships can become more resilient and nurturing.

Establishing boundaries is another critical aspect of healthy communication. Individuals with BPD often struggle with feelings of abandonment and intense emotional reactions, making it essential for both parties to articulate their needs and limits clearly. Encouraging open discussions about boundaries fosters mutual respect and can help prevent conflicts from escalating. Family members and friends should feel empowered to express their boundaries while also being sensitive to the emotional landscape of their loved ones. This balance is key to maintaining healthy dynamics and ensuring that both parties feel safe and valued.

Understanding BPD: A Resource Guide for Families and Friends

Using "I" statements can further enhance communication by reducing defensiveness and promoting constructive dialogue. Instead of saying, "You never listen to me," a more effective approach would be, "I feel unheard when our conversations get interrupted." This technique allows individuals to express their feelings without placing blame, making it easier for the other person to respond positively. Practicing "I" statements can lead to more productive conversations and help prevent the escalation of conflicts, particularly during emotionally charged discussions.

Lastly, practicing mindfulness in communication can greatly improve interactions. By being present and fully engaged in conversations, individuals can better manage their emotions and reactions. Mindfulness techniques, such as deep breathing or taking a moment to reflect before responding, can help individuals with BPD navigate challenging conversations with greater ease. This practice not only benefits those with BPD but also encourages family members and friends to approach discussions with patience and understanding. Building communication skills through mindfulness ultimately creates a foundation for healthier relationships, fostering an environment of support and empathy.

Setting Boundaries and Expectations

Setting boundaries and expectations is essential for individuals with borderline personality disorder (BPD), their families, and friends. Establishing clear boundaries helps create a sense of safety and stability in relationships, which is particularly important given the emotional volatility often associated with BPD. For individuals with BPD, understanding personal boundaries can significantly contribute to emotional regulation. It allows them to identify their limits and communicate their needs effectively, reducing feelings of overwhelm and abandonment that can arise in interpersonal interactions.

Family members and friends play a crucial role in this process by modeling healthy boundary-setting behaviors. It is vital for them to communicate their own boundaries clearly and consistently. This not only protects their emotional well-being but also teaches individuals with BPD the importance of mutual respect in relationships. By openly discussing expectations around communication, availability, and emotional support, families can foster an environment where everyone feels respected and understood. This collaborative approach can significantly improve the dynamics of relationships affected by BPD.

Understanding BPD: A Resource Guide for Families and Friends

To set effective boundaries, it is helpful to utilize specific techniques that promote understanding and respect. One such technique is the use of "I" statements, which encourage individuals to express their feelings and needs without placing blame or creating defensiveness in others. For example, saying "I feel overwhelmed when conversations become heated" is more constructive than "You always make me feel anxious." This approach not only clarifies personal feelings but also invites dialogue about boundaries without escalating tensions.

In addition to verbal communication, written agreements can be beneficial for setting expectations. Creating a document that outlines mutual boundaries and responsibilities can serve as a reference point to reduce misunderstandings. This written format can also be revisited regularly, allowing for adjustments as relationships evolve. Such tools can empower individuals with BPD to take an active role in shaping their interactions, fostering a sense of agency that is often essential for emotional well-being.

Understanding BPD: A Resource Guide for Families and Friends

Lastly, it is important to recognize that setting boundaries is an ongoing process that requires patience and flexibility. Individuals with BPD, family members, and friends should be prepared for adjustments as situations change. Regular check-ins can help maintain clarity and reinforce the importance of boundaries in nurturing healthy relationships. By cultivating an environment where boundaries are respected and expectations are clear, all parties can contribute to a supportive network that enhances emotional regulation and overall well-being for those affected by borderline personality disorder.

Understanding BPD: A Resource Guide for Families and Friends

Understanding BPD: A Resource Guide for Families and Friends

Chapter 6

Creative Therapies for Self-Expression

Art Therapy Techniques

Art therapy techniques offer a unique avenue for individuals with borderline personality disorder (BPD) to explore their emotions and experiences in a non-verbal manner. This approach allows individuals to express feelings that may be difficult to articulate, enabling a deeper understanding of their emotional landscapes. Art therapy can serve as a powerful tool for emotional regulation, providing a safe space where individuals can process complex emotions, reduce anxiety, and enhance self-awareness. Through various mediums such as drawing, painting, or sculpture, participants can externalize their internal struggles, which often leads to insights that contribute to their therapeutic journey.

Understanding BPD: A Resource Guide for Families and Friends

One effective technique within art therapy is guided imagery, where therapists encourage individuals to visualize a calming scene or an ideal self. Following this visualization, participants create artwork that reflects their experience. This process can help individuals with BPD identify and articulate their feelings related to self-image and self-worth. By visually representing their thoughts and emotions, they can gain a clearer perspective on their challenges and begin to develop healthier coping strategies. This technique promotes emotional regulation by facilitating a dialogue between the individual and their artwork, creating an opportunity for reflection and healing.

Another valuable art therapy technique is journaling through art, which combines traditional journaling with creative expression. Individuals can draw, collage, or paint in response to prompts related to their daily experiences, emotional triggers, or interpersonal relationships. This method encourages the exploration of feelings associated with BPD, such as fear of abandonment or emotional instability, while also fostering a sense of accomplishment and ownership over their narrative. By documenting their emotions visually, individuals can track their progress over time, recognizing patterns and gaining insights that can inform their therapeutic work.

Understanding BPD: A Resource Guide for Families and Friends

Collaborative art projects can also be beneficial for those with BPD, particularly in fostering connection and understanding within support systems. Engaging in group art therapy encourages communication and teamwork, allowing individuals to share their experiences in a supportive environment. This technique not only enhances social skills but also reinforces the importance of healthy relationships, which are often a significant challenge for those with BPD. Participants learn to navigate interpersonal dynamics in a creative context, promoting empathy and reducing feelings of isolation.

Incorporating art therapy techniques into a broader therapeutic framework can enhance overall emotional well-being for individuals with BPD. These creative methods complement traditional therapeutic approaches and can be particularly effective when combined with mindfulness practices and self-help strategies. By integrating art therapy into their daily routine, individuals can develop a more profound understanding of their emotions, improve their coping mechanisms, and foster healthier relationships. For families and friends, understanding these techniques can promote supportive conversations and encourage the practice of creative expression as a form of healing.

Writing and Journaling as Healing Tools

Writing and journaling can serve as powerful healing tools for individuals grappling with borderline personality disorder (BPD). These practices offer a safe space for self-expression, allowing individuals to articulate thoughts and feelings that may otherwise remain unprocessed. Writing helps to externalize internal struggles, transforming chaotic emotions into coherent narratives. This process can be particularly beneficial for those with BPD, as it fosters a sense of control over overwhelming feelings and provides clarity during turbulent times.

Engaging in regular journaling can also enhance emotional regulation, a key area of difficulty for those with BPD. By documenting emotional experiences, individuals can begin to identify patterns in their thoughts and behaviors. This reflective practice facilitates a deeper understanding of emotional triggers and responses, thereby promoting healthier coping strategies. Over time, journaling can help individuals develop skills to manage their emotions in real time, reducing impulsivity and fostering resilience.

Understanding BPD: A Resource Guide for Families and Friends

Incorporating creative writing into journaling can further amplify its therapeutic effects. Creative expression allows individuals to explore complex emotions through various literary forms, such as poetry, short stories, or personal essays. This imaginative approach not only encourages self-discovery but also offers an avenue for exploring different perspectives on personal challenges. Creative writing can be particularly liberating, as it enables individuals to envision possibilities beyond their current struggles, fostering a sense of hope and empowerment.

For family members and friends of those with BPD, understanding and supporting the writing and journaling process can enhance relational dynamics. Encouragement of journaling as a form of self-care shows a commitment to the individual's healing journey. Additionally, discussing journal entries can create opportunities for deeper conversations and connection, allowing loved ones to gain insight into the individual's experiences. This collaborative approach can strengthen relationships and provide a supportive environment conducive to healing.

Mental health professionals can integrate writing and journaling techniques into therapeutic practices for individuals with BPD. Guided journal prompts and structured writing exercises can be employed to facilitate self-exploration and emotional processing within therapy sessions. By incorporating these tools, professionals can enhance engagement and provide clients with tangible resources to navigate their emotional landscape. Ultimately, writing and journaling not only serve as vehicles for self-expression but also foster a sense of agency and empowerment in the journey toward healing and recovery.

Music and Movement Therapies

Music and movement therapies have emerged as effective interventions for individuals with borderline personality disorder (BPD), providing unique avenues for emotional expression and regulation. These therapies harness the power of rhythm, melody, and physical movement to create a safe space for self-exploration and healing. For those struggling with the intense emotions characteristic of BPD, engaging in music and movement can facilitate a deeper connection to one's feelings while promoting relaxation and mindfulness. This subchapter will explore how these therapies can be integrated into the coping strategies for emotional regulation and overall well-being.

Understanding BPD: A Resource Guide for Families and Friends

Music therapy typically involves the use of music to address emotional, cognitive, and social needs. Through listening, songwriting, and improvisation, individuals can express feelings that may be difficult to articulate verbally. For individuals with BPD, where emotions can be particularly volatile, music therapy offers an outlet that can help them process these feelings in a constructive way. Participating in group music therapy sessions can also foster a sense of community and belonging, which is crucial for those who may feel isolated due to their disorder. By sharing musical experiences, individuals can develop healthier relationships and improve their interpersonal skills.

Movement therapy, which encompasses approaches such as dance and expressive movement, provides another powerful tool for emotional regulation. This form of therapy encourages individuals to explore their emotions through body movement, allowing for the release of pent-up tension and fostering a sense of physical and emotional grounding. For someone with BPD, movement therapy can help cultivate awareness of bodily sensations and emotional states, promoting mindfulness and self-acceptance. By integrating movement into their coping strategies, individuals can learn to recognize and manage their emotional responses more effectively.

Understanding BPD: A Resource Guide for Families and Friends

The combination of music and movement therapies can be particularly beneficial for individuals with co-occurring disorders, such as anxiety and depression. These therapies are nonverbal, making them suitable for those who struggle with communication due to overwhelming emotions. Engaging in creative expression can serve as a form of self-soothing and distraction, helping to mitigate the impact of distressing symptoms. Additionally, these therapeutic modalities can complement traditional talk therapies, providing a holistic approach to treatment that addresses both psychological and physiological aspects of BPD.

Families and friends of individuals with BPD can also benefit from understanding and supporting the use of music and movement therapies. Encouraging participation in these therapeutic activities can enhance the emotional well-being of their loved ones and foster healthier relationships. By exploring local resources such as community centers, therapists specializing in creative arts, or online programs, families can help individuals with BPD find suitable avenues for expression and healing. As they navigate the complexities of BPD together, incorporating music and movement therapies can enrich the support system and encourage ongoing personal development.

Understanding BPD: A Resource Guide for Families and Friends

Understanding BPD: A Resource Guide for Families and Friends

Chapter 7

Navigating Therapy Options

Types of Therapy for BPD

Borderline Personality Disorder (BPD) can often feel overwhelming, not just for those living with the condition but also for their families and friends. Fortunately, various therapeutic approaches are designed to help individuals manage their symptoms and build healthier relationships. Understanding these different types of therapy can empower those affected by BPD to find the right support that aligns with their unique needs and circumstances.

Dialectical Behavior Therapy (DBT) is one of the most well-researched and effective treatments for BPD. Developed by Dr. Marsha Linehan, DBT combines cognitive-behavioral techniques with mindfulness practices. The therapy focuses on teaching skills in four key areas: emotional regulation, distress tolerance, interpersonal effectiveness, and mindfulness. By learning how to manage intense emotions and improve relationships, individuals can reduce impulsive behaviors and develop a more stable sense of self. Families and friends can also benefit from DBT, as it encourages open communication and understanding within relationships.

Understanding BPD: A Resource Guide for Families and Friends

Mentalization-Based Therapy (MBT) is another therapeutic approach that aims to enhance an individual's ability to understand their own thoughts and feelings, as well as those of others. This therapy focuses on improving the capacity to reflect on mental states, which can be particularly challenging for individuals with BPD. By fostering greater insight into emotional experiences and interpersonal dynamics, MBT helps individuals develop healthier coping strategies and improve their ability to relate to others. For families and friends, understanding the principles of MBT can facilitate better support and communication with their loved ones.

Schema-Focused Therapy is a therapeutic approach that combines cognitive-behavioral techniques with an understanding of early life experiences and their impact on current behavior. This therapy identifies and modifies deeply ingrained patterns, or schemas, that contribute to the challenges faced by individuals with BPD. By recognizing these schemas, individuals can begin to challenge negative thought patterns and develop healthier ways of thinking and behaving. Family members are encouraged to engage in the therapeutic process, as their involvement can reinforce positive changes and provide a supportive environment for recovery.

Creative therapies, including art therapy and music therapy, offer alternative avenues for self-expression and healing for those with BPD. These modalities encourage individuals to explore their emotions and experiences in non-verbal ways, which can be particularly beneficial for those who struggle to articulate their feelings. Engaging in creative activities can help reduce anxiety and foster a sense of accomplishment and self-worth. Families and friends can support their loved ones by participating in creative activities together, promoting bonding and understanding in a non-threatening environment.

Finding the Right Therapist

Finding the right therapist is a crucial step for individuals with borderline personality disorder (BPD) and their families. The therapeutic relationship can significantly impact the treatment journey, making it essential to choose someone who understands BPD and employs effective strategies tailored to the unique challenges associated with the disorder. Start by considering therapists who have specialized training in BPD and related emotional regulation strategies. Many professionals will list their areas of expertise on their websites or profiles, allowing individuals to refine their search based on specific needs and therapeutic approaches.

Understanding BPD: A Resource Guide for Families and Friends

When exploring potential therapists, it is vital to consider their therapeutic modalities. Dialectical behavior therapy (DBT) is widely recognized as one of the most effective treatments for BPD, focusing on skill-building in areas such as emotional regulation, interpersonal effectiveness, and distress tolerance. However, other therapies, such as cognitive-behavioral therapy (CBT), schema therapy, and mindfulness-based approaches, may also be beneficial. Understanding these modalities can help individuals identify which aligns best with their preferences and goals. It's also important to remember that a therapist's approach should be adaptable, as needs may evolve over time.

Another critical aspect of finding the right therapist involves the interpersonal dynamic between the therapist and the client. A strong therapeutic alliance is foundational for effective treatment. During initial consultations, pay attention to the therapist's communication style, empathy, and ability to connect. Feeling safe and understood is essential for fostering open dialogue about emotions and experiences. If the initial fit does not feel right, it is perfectly acceptable to seek out additional options. The process of finding a therapist who resonates personally can be an integral part of the healing journey.

Understanding BPD: A Resource Guide for Families and Friends

Logistics, such as location, accessibility, and cost, can also influence the choice of therapist. Consider whether in-person sessions or online therapy would work better for your schedule and comfort level. Additionally, check if the therapist accepts insurance or offers sliding scale fees to accommodate different financial situations. Understanding these practical aspects can alleviate stress and enable individuals to focus on the therapeutic process itself.

Lastly, it is beneficial to involve family members and friends in the conversation about therapy, as their support can be invaluable. Educating loved ones about BPD and the various therapeutic options available helps create a more informed support system. Resources such as support groups, educational workshops, and community outreach programs can provide additional guidance in navigating this journey. Ultimately, finding the right therapist is a personalized process that requires time, patience, and self-reflection, but the right match can lead to profound emotional growth and healing.

The Role of Family in Therapy

The role of family in therapy for individuals with borderline personality disorder (BPD) is crucial, as the family unit often serves as a primary support system. Family members can provide emotional stability and understanding, which are essential for someone navigating the complexities of BPD. In therapy, families can learn about the disorder, its symptoms, and the impact it has on behavior and relationships. This knowledge helps them develop empathy and patience, fostering an environment where the individual feels safe to express themselves and work through their challenges.

Involving family in therapy sessions can enhance the therapeutic process. It allows for open communication between the individual and their family members, helping to clarify misunderstandings and reduce conflict. Family therapy can address relational dynamics, improve communication skills, and establish healthy boundaries. This collaborative approach encourages families to participate actively in the healing process, demonstrating that recovery is a shared journey rather than an isolated experience.

Understanding BPD: A Resource Guide for Families and Friends

Coping strategies for emotional regulation are often discussed in family therapy, equipping both the individual and their family with tools to manage intense emotions. Families can learn to recognize triggers and develop strategies to respond effectively. By practicing these skills together, family members not only support their loved one but also reinforce their own emotional resilience. This mutual learning process can enhance relationships and create a more harmonious home environment, which is beneficial for everyone involved.

Nutrition and meal planning can also play a role in family therapy. Families can work together to create balanced meal plans that support the individual's mental health. Understanding the connection between nutrition and emotional well-being can empower families to make healthier choices as a unit. This shared responsibility promotes teamwork and accountability, fostering a sense of unity and purpose in the recovery process.

Finally, families can benefit from community resources and support systems designed for those affected by BPD. Engaging with local or online support groups provides families with additional perspectives and coping strategies. These resources can also offer education about BPD, enhancing the family's ability to support their loved one effectively. By harnessing the strengths of the family unit and external resources, individuals with BPD can experience a more supportive and understanding environment, facilitating their journey toward healing and stability.

Understanding BPD: A Resource Guide for Families and Friends

Understanding BPD: A Resource Guide for Families and Friends

Chapter 8

Support Systems and Community Resources

Importance of Support Networks

Support networks play a crucial role in the lives of individuals with borderline personality disorder (BPD), providing a foundation for emotional stability, understanding, and resilience. These networks can include family members, friends, mental health professionals, and peer support groups, each contributing to a multifaceted support system. For individuals with BPD, having a reliable support network can significantly influence their ability to manage symptoms, navigate challenges, and pursue personal growth. This network not only helps in mitigating feelings of isolation but also fosters a sense of belonging and connection, which is essential for emotional well-being.

Understanding BPD: A Resource Guide for Families and Friends

Family and friends form the core of an individual's support network, offering love, understanding, and acceptance. Their presence can serve as a buffer against the intense emotional fluctuations that often accompany BPD. When family members and friends educate themselves about the disorder, they can respond with empathy rather than frustration, helping to create a safe environment for open communication. This supportive atmosphere encourages individuals with BPD to express their feelings and seek help when needed, reinforcing the importance of healthy relationships for emotional regulation and resilience.

Mental health professionals also play a vital role in the support network. They provide structured guidance through therapy and counseling, equipping individuals with coping strategies to manage emotional dysregulation. Moreover, mental health professionals can facilitate connections to community resources, such as support groups and workshops, which can enhance an individual's coping toolkit. Through these relationships, individuals with BPD can gain insights into their experiences and learn effective techniques for managing symptoms, thereby fostering a sense of empowerment and agency in their recovery journey.

Understanding BPD: A Resource Guide for Families and Friends

Peer support groups are another essential component of a robust support network. These groups offer a unique space for individuals with BPD to share their experiences and learn from one another. The validation that comes from connecting with others who understand similar struggles can be incredibly healing. Sharing coping strategies, mindfulness techniques, and personal stories fosters a sense of community and reduces feelings of isolation. In addition, these groups can serve as a platform for creative expression and healing, allowing individuals to explore their emotions in a supportive environment.

Building and maintaining a strong support network requires effort and commitment from both the individual with BPD and their loved ones. It involves open communication about needs, boundaries, and expectations. Encouraging family members and friends to participate in educational resources can further strengthen their ability to provide effective support. By actively engaging in a network of understanding and compassion, individuals with BPD can cultivate healthier relationships and enhance their overall quality of life, ultimately navigating their journey toward recovery with greater confidence and resilience.

Finding Local Resources

Finding local resources is a crucial step for individuals with borderline personality disorder (BPD) and their families. These resources can play a significant role in providing support, education, and coping strategies. Local resources may include mental health professionals, support groups, community centers, and educational workshops. Each of these can offer tailored assistance that aligns with the unique challenges faced by those living with BPD. Connecting with these resources can help individuals better understand their condition, develop coping strategies, and foster healthier relationships.

Mental health professionals in your area can provide valuable guidance for managing BPD. Psychiatrists, therapists, and counselors who specialize in personality disorders are essential for effective treatment. They can offer individual therapy, group therapy, or family sessions that focus on emotional regulation, mindfulness, and coping mechanisms. It's important to research and find professionals who have experience with BPD, as their understanding of the disorder can greatly influence the effectiveness of treatment. Many practitioners also offer sliding scale fees or work with insurance companies, making it more accessible for families and individuals seeking help.

Understanding BPD: A Resource Guide for Families and Friends

Support groups provide a space for individuals with BPD and their loved ones to share experiences and strategies. Local chapters of national organizations often host regular meetings where participants can connect with others facing similar challenges. These gatherings can foster a sense of community and reduce feelings of isolation. Additionally, family members can benefit from separate support groups designed to help them understand BPD better and learn how to support their loved one effectively. Engaging in these groups can enhance emotional resilience and provide practical tools for navigating daily challenges.

Community centers often offer workshops and classes focused on skills development for emotional regulation, mindfulness, and self-care. These programs may include activities such as art therapy, yoga, or meditation, all of which can be beneficial for individuals with BPD. Nutrition and meal planning workshops can also be found at local health centers, emphasizing the connection between diet and emotional well-being. By participating in these activities, individuals can learn new coping strategies and build a supportive network with others who share similar experiences.

Finally, educational resources tailored for families and friends of those with BPD can be invaluable. Libraries, local universities, and mental health organizations often provide literature and workshops that help loved ones understand the nuances of BPD. These resources can empower families to create a supportive environment and foster healthier relationships. Furthermore, staying informed about co-occurring disorders and their management is essential for a holistic approach to treatment. By actively seeking out local resources, individuals and families can cultivate a comprehensive support system that enhances recovery and promotes well-being.

Online Support Communities

Online support communities have emerged as invaluable resources for individuals with borderline personality disorder (BPD), their families, and mental health professionals. These virtual spaces provide a platform for members to share experiences, offer advice, and foster connections with others who understand the challenges associated with BPD. The anonymity of the internet allows individuals to engage at their own comfort level, making it easier to discuss sensitive topics related to emotional regulation, relationships, and coping strategies without fear of judgment.

Understanding BPD: A Resource Guide for Families and Friends

One of the key benefits of online support communities is the opportunity for members to exchange coping strategies for emotional regulation. Individuals with BPD often experience intense emotions that can feel overwhelming. In these communities, members can share specific techniques that have worked for them, such as grounding exercises, mindfulness practices, and breathing exercises. By learning from the successes and struggles of others, participants can build their own toolkit for managing emotional distress, which can significantly enhance their quality of life.

Nutrition and meal planning also play a crucial role in managing BPD symptoms, and online support groups often discuss these topics as well. Healthy eating can impact mood and overall mental well-being. Members can share recipes, meal prep ideas, and tips for making nutritious choices that support emotional stability. By fostering a discussion about nutrition, these communities help members understand the connection between what they eat and how they feel, promoting healthier lifestyle choices that can contribute to managing BPD.

Understanding BPD: A Resource Guide for Families and Friends

Building healthy relationships is another critical area of focus within online support communities. Individuals with BPD may struggle with interpersonal relationships due to fear of abandonment or intense emotional reactions. Through shared stories and advice, community members can learn how to navigate relationships more effectively, develop communication skills, and set boundaries. This support can empower individuals to foster more stable and fulfilling connections with family, friends, and romantic partners, ultimately improving their social support networks.

Lastly, online support communities serve as a bridge to educational resources and therapy options. Members often share information about local therapists, workshops, and self-help resources that have proven beneficial. They can discuss various therapeutic approaches, such as dialectical behavior therapy (DBT) and creative therapies, which can offer new avenues for self-expression and healing. By providing access to a wealth of knowledge and resources, these communities help individuals with BPD and their loved ones make informed decisions about their mental health journeys.

Understanding BPD: A Resource Guide for Families and Friends

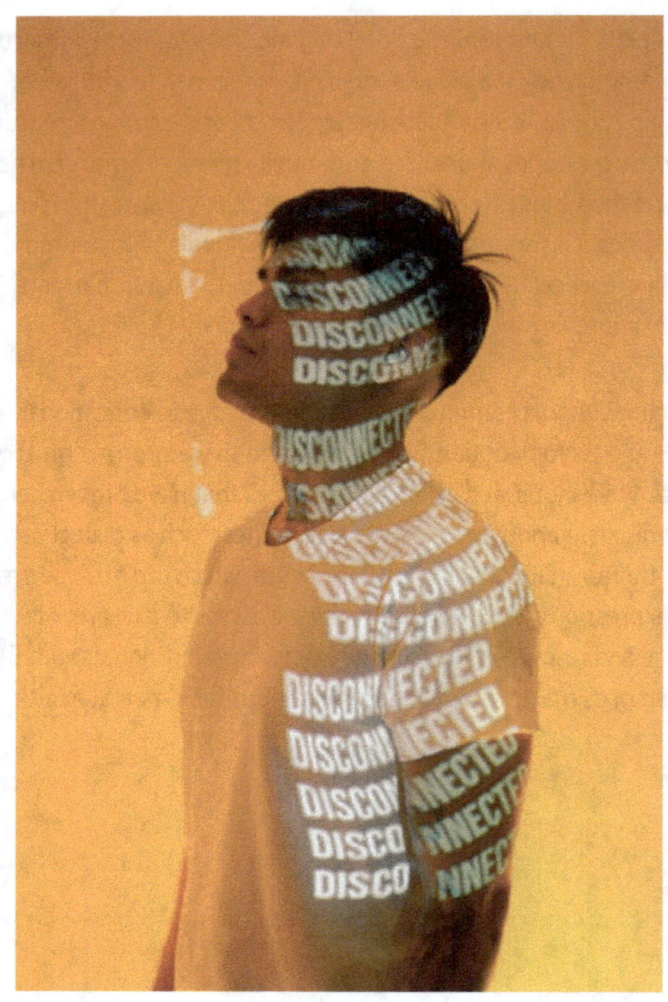

Understanding BPD: A Resource Guide for Families and Friends

Chapter 9

Managing Co-occurring Disorders

Understanding Co-occurring Conditions

Understanding co-occurring conditions is crucial when addressing borderline personality disorder (BPD) as many individuals with BPD also experience additional mental health disorders. These co-occurring conditions can complicate diagnosis, treatment, and recovery, making it essential for families, friends, and mental health professionals to recognize and understand the interplay between BPD and other disorders. Common co-occurring conditions include depression, anxiety disorders, substance use disorders, and post-traumatic stress disorder (PTSD). Each of these can exacerbate the symptoms of BPD, leading to increased emotional dysregulation and interpersonal challenges.

Understanding BPD: A Resource Guide for Families and Friends

The presence of co-occurring disorders often affects the emotional regulation strategies that individuals with BPD may employ. For instance, anxiety can heighten feelings of panic and abandonment, intensifying the emotional swings typical of BPD. Conversely, depression may lead to withdrawal from relationships and activities that could provide support, resulting in isolation and exacerbation of BPD symptoms. Understanding these dynamics allows family members and friends to provide more targeted support and encourages mental health professionals to develop comprehensive treatment plans that address all underlying issues rather than focusing solely on BPD.

Nutrition and lifestyle choices also play a critical role in managing co-occurring conditions. Individuals with BPD may benefit from meal planning strategies that promote overall mental health, such as incorporating omega-3 fatty acids and reducing sugar intake. A balanced diet can help stabilize mood and improve emotional resilience. Additionally, mindfulness and meditation techniques can be particularly effective in managing both BPD and co-occurring disorders like anxiety and depression. These practices foster a greater awareness of one's thoughts and feelings, providing tools to cope with emotional upheaval and promoting a sense of calm.

Understanding BPD: A Resource Guide for Families and Friends

Building healthy relationships is another vital aspect of managing co-occurring conditions alongside BPD. Individuals may struggle with trust and emotional intimacy due to their BPD symptoms, which can be further complicated by other disorders like PTSD. Encouraging open communication and establishing boundaries can help create a safe space for both the individual with BPD and their loved ones. Support systems, including therapy groups or community resources, can provide the necessary encouragement and understanding that foster healing and connection.

Navigating therapy options is essential for those dealing with BPD and co-occurring disorders. Integrated treatment approaches that address all aspects of an individual's mental health can significantly enhance recovery outcomes. This might include combining dialectical behavior therapy (DBT) with cognitive behavioral therapy (CBT) or exploring creative therapies for self-expression. Educational resources for families and friends can help them understand the complexities of co-occurring conditions, allowing them to better support their loved ones. By fostering an environment of understanding and support, individuals with BPD can work toward healing and improved overall well-being.

Integrated Treatment Approaches

Integrated treatment approaches for borderline personality disorder (BPD) emphasize the necessity of combining various therapeutic modalities to address the multifaceted nature of the disorder. Individuals with BPD often experience intense emotional fluctuations, difficulty in relationships, and challenges with self-image. Therefore, a comprehensive treatment plan that encompasses psychotherapy, medication, nutritional support, and mindfulness practices can significantly enhance emotional regulation and overall well-being. By recognizing the interplay of these elements, individuals, families, and mental health professionals can work together to create a more effective treatment strategy.

Psychotherapy remains the cornerstone of treatment for BPD, with dialectical behavior therapy (DBT) being one of the most researched and effective approaches. DBT focuses on skills training in areas such as emotional regulation, distress tolerance, interpersonal effectiveness, and mindfulness. However, integrating other therapeutic modalities can offer additional benefits. For instance, cognitive-behavioral therapy (CBT) can help individuals identify and challenge distorted thought patterns that contribute to emotional dysregulation. Moreover, creative therapies, such as art and music therapy, can provide alternative avenues for self-expression, allowing individuals to articulate feelings that may be difficult to verbalize.

Understanding BPD: A Resource Guide for Families and Friends

Nutrition and meal planning play a crucial role in managing BPD symptoms. A well-balanced diet can positively impact mood and energy levels, aiding in emotional regulation. Professionals can work with individuals to develop personalized meal plans that incorporate nutrient-dense foods, promoting overall mental health. Additionally, educating families and friends about the significance of nutrition can foster a supportive environment where healthy eating habits are encouraged. Understanding how food choices affect mood can empower individuals with BPD to make more informed decisions regarding their diet.

Mindfulness and meditation techniques tailored for individuals with BPD can further enhance emotional stability. These practices encourage present-moment awareness and acceptance, which can help individuals recognize and manage their emotional responses more effectively. Techniques such as guided imagery, deep breathing exercises, and body scans can serve as valuable tools in moments of distress. Families and friends can also benefit from mindfulness practices, as they can learn to remain calm and present when supporting their loved ones, reducing the overall tension in relationships.

Building healthy relationships is essential for individuals with BPD, and integrated treatment approaches can facilitate this process. Therapeutic settings can provide opportunities for role-playing and practicing social skills, enabling individuals to engage more positively with others. Support systems, including peer groups and community resources, can further enhance this learning experience by creating environments where individuals feel understood and validated. By combining these diverse strategies, integrated treatment approaches can promote healing and resilience, helping individuals with BPD lead fulfilling lives while fostering supportive relationships with their families and friends.

Support Strategies for Co-occurring Disorders

Support strategies for individuals with co-occurring disorders, particularly in the context of borderline personality disorder (BPD), require a multifaceted approach that addresses both mental health and any additional issues such as substance use, anxiety, or depression. Understanding that BPD can often coexist with other disorders is crucial for developing effective treatment plans. Integrated care that combines psychological support, medical treatment, and community resources can significantly enhance the quality of life for those affected. This collaborative approach engages various healthcare professionals, ensuring that individuals receive comprehensive support tailored to their unique needs.

Understanding BPD: A Resource Guide for Families and Friends

Emotional regulation remains a central challenge for those with BPD and co-occurring disorders. Coping strategies that focus on mindfulness and emotional awareness can be particularly beneficial. Techniques such as grounding exercises, deep breathing, and guided imagery help individuals manage distressing emotions and reduce impulsive reactions. Incorporating these practices into daily routines not only aids emotional stability but also enhances the effectiveness of therapy. Mental health professionals can facilitate this process by providing structured guidance and resources, encouraging individuals to explore the benefits of mindfulness in a safe and supportive environment.

Nutrition and meal planning also play a significant role in the overall well-being of individuals with BPD and co-occurring disorders. Nutritional imbalances can exacerbate emotional dysregulation, making it essential to focus on a balanced diet that supports mental health. Education on how certain foods affect mood and energy levels can empower individuals to make healthier choices. For families and friends, understanding the importance of nutrition can be a vital component of support. They can assist in meal planning and preparation, fostering a sense of community and shared responsibility that promotes healthier habits.

Understanding BPD: A Resource Guide for Families and Friends

Building healthy relationships is another critical support strategy. Individuals with BPD often struggle with interpersonal dynamics, which can become even more complicated when co-occurring disorders are present. Establishing clear communication, setting boundaries, and practicing active listening are essential skills that can be developed through therapy and support groups. These skills not only facilitate healthier interactions but also instill a sense of trust and safety in relationships. Family and friends can play a pivotal role by participating in educational workshops or support networks, learning how to best support their loved ones while also taking care of their own emotional needs.

Lastly, connecting with community resources and support systems is paramount for managing co-occurring disorders alongside BPD. Access to peer support groups, educational workshops, and crisis intervention services can provide individuals and their families with vital tools and networks. These resources help reduce feelings of isolation and promote a sense of belonging. Mental health professionals can guide individuals in navigating these community options, ensuring that they receive the comprehensive support necessary for recovery. By fostering a collaborative approach that combines individual therapy, community resources, and education, individuals with BPD and co-occurring disorders can cultivate resilience and enhance their overall quality of life.

Understanding BPD: A Resource Guide for Families and Friends

Understanding BPD: A Resource Guide for Families and Friends

Chapter 10

Educational Resources for Families and Friends

Understanding BPD from a Family Perspective

Understanding borderline personality disorder (BPD) from a family perspective involves recognizing the complexities of the disorder and its impact on relationships. Families often navigate a labyrinth of emotions when a loved one is diagnosed with BPD. This journey can be overwhelming, as family members grapple with feelings of confusion, frustration, and helplessness. Understanding the symptoms and behaviors associated with BPD, such as intense emotional fluctuations, fear of abandonment, and difficulties in interpersonal relationships, can help families foster empathy and patience. By gaining insight into these experiences, families can develop healthier communication patterns and create supportive environments that promote healing.

Understanding BPD: A Resource Guide for Families and Friends

Coping strategies play a crucial role in managing the emotional turmoil that often accompanies BPD. Families can benefit from learning about emotional regulation techniques that their loved ones can practice. Encouraging mindfulness and meditation can be particularly effective, as these practices help individuals with BPD to ground themselves during moments of crisis. Families can also engage in these techniques together, fostering a sense of unity and shared understanding. By establishing routines that incorporate healthy meal planning and nutrition, families can support their loved ones in maintaining physical health, which is deeply intertwined with emotional well-being.

Building healthy relationships is essential for both individuals with BPD and their families. Open communication, setting boundaries, and practicing active listening are vital skills that can enhance interactions and reduce misunderstandings. Families should be encouraged to express their feelings honestly while also being sensitive to the emotional state of their loved one. This reciprocal approach can help mitigate the fear of abandonment that individuals with BPD often experience. It's important for families to recognize that while they can provide support, they must also take care of their own emotional needs to maintain a balanced dynamic.

Understanding BPD: A Resource Guide for Families and Friends

Creative therapies can serve as powerful outlets for self-expression and healing for individuals with BPD. Families can explore art therapy, music therapy, or writing as a means of facilitating emotional expression in a safe environment. Encouraging participation in these activities not only provides a constructive way to cope with feelings but also creates opportunities for family bonding. Engaging in creative pursuits together can help break down barriers, allowing families to connect on a deeper level, while also providing their loved ones with tools to articulate their emotions more effectively.

Navigating therapy options is another critical aspect of understanding BPD from a family perspective. Families should be informed about the various therapeutic approaches available, such as dialectical behavior therapy (DBT), cognitive-behavioral therapy (CBT), and others. Familiarity with these therapies can empower families to make informed decisions about treatment and support their loved ones in seeking appropriate help. Additionally, building a support system and accessing community resources can alleviate some of the burdens associated with BPD. Establishing connections with support groups, educational resources, and mental health professionals can offer families the guidance and understanding they need to effectively support their loved ones while also fostering their own resilience.

Books and Online Resources

Books and online resources serve as vital tools for individuals navigating the complexities of borderline personality disorder (BPD). Numerous publications delve into the intricacies of emotional regulation, providing readers with coping strategies that can be essential for managing intense emotions. Titles such as "The Emotion Regulation Skills System for Cognitively Challenged Clients" offer practical exercises and insights tailored for those with BPD. These resources emphasize the importance of understanding emotional triggers and developing skills to respond to them effectively, thus empowering individuals to achieve a greater sense of stability.

Nutrition plays a significant role in mental health, and various resources address the connection between diet and emotional well-being. Books like "The Mindful Diet" explore how nutrition impacts mood and behavior, offering meal planning strategies that support emotional regulation. Resources focusing on BPD often highlight the importance of balanced nutrition, emphasizing whole foods and the reduction of processed items that may exacerbate emotional disturbances. By integrating nutritional knowledge into daily routines, individuals can enhance their overall mental health and bolster their coping mechanisms.

Understanding BPD: A Resource Guide for Families and Friends

Mindfulness and meditation are powerful practices for individuals with BPD, and a wealth of literature exists on these topics. Works such as "The Mindfulness Workbook for BPD" provide guided exercises aimed at fostering awareness and acceptance of one's emotional experience. Online platforms also offer guided meditations specifically designed for those with BPD, helping individuals cultivate a sense of calm and presence. Engaging with these resources can significantly improve emotional regulation, enabling individuals to respond to stressors with greater resilience.

Building healthy relationships is crucial for individuals with BPD, and numerous books and online guides focus on this aspect of recovery. Titles like "I Hate You—Don't Leave Me" discuss the challenges of interpersonal relationships while providing strategies for establishing and maintaining healthy connections. Online forums and support groups also serve as valuable resources, allowing individuals to share experiences and gain insights from others who understand the complexities of BPD. These relationships can create a sense of community, which is essential for healing and growth.

Lastly, for those navigating therapy options and co-occurring disorders, educational resources are invaluable. Books that outline various therapeutic approaches, such as dialectical behavior therapy (DBT) and schema therapy, help individuals and their families understand treatment pathways. Online resources, including databases and directories of mental health professionals, assist in finding appropriate care. Additionally, materials focusing on co-occurring disorders provide insights into managing multiple challenges simultaneously, ensuring that individuals receive comprehensive support tailored to their unique situations.

Workshops and Support Groups

Workshops and support groups serve as vital resources for individuals with borderline personality disorder (BPD) and their families. These gatherings provide a safe environment where participants can share experiences, gain insights, and learn coping strategies tailored to the unique challenges posed by BPD. By engaging in workshops focused on emotional regulation, attendees can explore various techniques to manage intense feelings effectively. Such sessions often include interactive components, allowing participants to practice mindfulness exercises and learn about nutrition's role in emotional wellbeing, helping them to establish healthier eating habits that support their mental health.

Understanding BPD: A Resource Guide for Families and Friends

Support groups play a crucial role in building a sense of community among individuals with BPD and their loved ones. These groups foster open communication, allowing members to express their thoughts and feelings without judgment. Participants can share personal experiences regarding their struggles and triumphs, creating a powerful bond that alleviates feelings of isolation. Furthermore, family members can gain valuable perspectives on their loved one's experiences, which can enhance understanding and empathy within the family dynamic. This mutual support is essential for nurturing healthy relationships amidst the challenges of living with BPD.

Workshops often incorporate mindfulness and meditation techniques specifically designed for those with BPD. Practicing mindfulness can help individuals become more aware of their emotions and reactions, ultimately leading to greater emotional regulation. Guided meditations and breathing techniques taught in these sessions can empower participants to manage overwhelming feelings more effectively. Additionally, these practices encourage self-compassion, enabling individuals to approach their struggles with kindness rather than self-judgment, a critical component in the healing process.

Understanding BPD: A Resource Guide for Families and Friends

Creative therapies are another key focus in workshops and support groups dedicated to BPD. Activities such as art therapy, music therapy, and writing workshops provide alternative avenues for self-expression and healing. These creative outlets allow participants to explore their emotions in a non-verbal way, which can be particularly beneficial for those who find it difficult to articulate their feelings. Engaging in creative expression can also foster a sense of achievement and boost self-esteem, essential elements for individuals working towards recovery.

Navigating therapy options is also an essential topic covered in workshops and support groups. Mental health professionals can provide guidance on various therapeutic modalities that are effective for BPD, such as dialectical behavior therapy (DBT) and cognitive-behavioral therapy (CBT). By sharing resources and recommendations, these groups help individuals and their families identify the right therapeutic approaches for their specific needs. Additionally, discussions around managing co-occurring disorders, such as anxiety or substance use, are crucial for a comprehensive understanding of BPD, equipping attendees with knowledge and tools to seek appropriate support and treatment.